ABOVE THE BEJEWELED CITY

Jon Davis

Grid Books

Published by:

Grid Books
Boston, Massachusetts
grid-books.org

Copyright © 2021 by Jon Davis. Cover illustration copyright © 2013, 2021 by Dirk De Bruycker.
All rights reserved.

Cover painting: "The Longing," by Dirk De Bruycker, 2013, 84 in. x 72 in., mixed media on canvas.

Printed by Cushing–Malloy, Inc., Ann Arbor, Michigan. Book design by Michael Alpert.

ISBN 978-1-946830-13-5

ABOVE THE BEJEWELED CITY

ALSO BY JON DAVIS

BOOKS
An Amiable Reception for the Acrobat
Improbable Creatures
Heteronymy: An Anthology
Preliminary Report
Scrimmage of Appetite
Dangerous Amusements

CHAPBOOKS
Loving Horses
Thelonious Sphere
Local Color
The Hawk. The Road. The Sunlight After Clouds.
West of New England

TRANSLATIONS
Dayplaces, by Naseer Hassan

For my mother, Joan Carney Somers,

who started me on this journey

TABLE OF CONTENTS

Existence is inexplicable.

—Maurice Merleau-Ponty

ORALITY

"La luz del poeta es la contradicción."
–Federico García Lorca

A chattering in the acacias.
An extralinguistic taxonomy
of grasses. Seed-tuft. Absence.
Elision as lexical strategy. As in
this silence. This shrike. This
lizard pinned to barbed-wire.
Writhing. And the black *piñones*
crisp against a reddening sky.
A diorama made utterly of syllables,
of the pungent musk, the squalor
and demise, the archduke
of holding still. Still in darkness
and dew. The gaps and elisions,
plastered-over and jury-rigged.
The woman above the cistern,
silver and green and gone.
And the covert operations,
the Catholic and inscrutable,
the politics a wash of gray
over everything. The moon, now,
above the barren mountain.
That clarity. That fallacy.
The somnambulist, the only one
awake enough to see, to know—having
slumbered in the gorge, having
 crossed the Guadalquivir. The rooster

would have already crowed
from the cobblestone,
the *Guardia Civil* already clattered
down the moon-slick streets, batons
raised, their eyes obscured
by shadow and by shadow revealed,
the syntax a narrowing alley,
fewer doors, higher windows,
the climax and denouement assured,
the knife, the red rose blossoming
now as we always knew it would
on the white silk blouse.

RAIN

for Jean Valentine

I thought I held
a secret   something cached
at the edge   of a web

                if only
the words
would consent
           to shake it   to shape it

                the way a cloud
shapes a sky
           or ribbons   left to fray
shape a sparrow's nest

the words
           did not come
                the secret
           lost
                to wind & time

a salvation
           of sorts   since now
                we can step
off this yellow curb
                in rain
                      so lightly

THE WIND

For the longest time, the wind
only wanted some leaves,
an opportunity to shiver,
some long hair, some sun,
an opening to shine.
It wanted water, to stroke it
until it rose up and
rushed toward the sands,
the sands that the wind
had already been coaxing
gently into flight. But it wasn't
enough. All of it temporary,
ephemeral—the leaves,
the hair, the water. The sand,
kissed, not scarred. Touched,
not bruised. So the wind,
instead of blowing steadily,
lightly across the open,
abated, retreated, formulated
a new plan. It began whirling.
At first slowly, at sea,
for its own amusement. Then,
bored, it mounted the waves
and rode them shoreward,
where it shattered windows,
lifted roofs from buildings,
uprooted trees, scattered
toys and boards and plastic pools.

It mounded the water
and sent it crashing
into seawalls, swamped
the boatyard, cavorted
among the splendored yachts,
the dinghies moored
in the back bay. It had
no political aspirations,
no malice. It loved equally
each incidence of mayhem—
the tattered flags and banners,
the streetlights blasted
in their stanchions, flooded
basements and streets,
the old woman waving
from her rooftop
as the helicopter drifted
down. This wind
they would remember.
This wind they would name.
What more, the wind thought,
what more could one ask?

BIO NOTE

Borne past brick
and night-squall,
collared and frisked,
humdrumming
in the boom.
Credentialed by dawn
and to dawn indentured.
Briefly handsome
in the squalor, squalid
where hope met hoped-for.
Hopped-up. Hoveled.
Tenured. Muddled.
Tonsured by events,
spraddled and pratfallen,
labile in midlife,
fallow in the mudstruck eve.
Half grit, half grimace.
Leavened by sorrow,
joy but a glance.
Matriculating still,
long in the matrix
of gut and glyph.
Etched by circumstance
this stint on earth—

OF FROG OR FISH

That winter of the pandemic
when everything seemed mired
and maudlin—each day an arc
of mishearing and confusion,
everything prologue to a life
we kept projecting further
into a hazy future that, we hoped,
looked like the past: handshakes,
kisses, easy patter by the doorway,
long goodbyes in the drive,
unmasked sentiments.

I'd rented the neighbor's casita,
piled it with books and papers,
cords and computers, and set
to the drudgery of editing
and writing for pay. I leaned a ladder
against the fence on the far side
and clambered onto the potting table
on our side of the fence, then down
the ladder to the casita.

But I also had to attend
my stepson's illnesses, long nights
splayed on plastic chairs,
staring at oxygen, heart rate,
alarmed by beep and silence
and beep again. There was

a new emergency every month,
since this song was in that key,
and we had to listen all year.

But what I remember
most, when I let myself
remember, is the moment each
morning and again at sunset
when I climbed atop the ladder and stood
briefly above everything and saw,
past the neighbor's jumble of wires
and vent pipes, the cholla-choked
dirt lots that edged the dry riverbed:
the western sky, pale at dawn, bruised
red at dusk. And how I thought,
one night, stepping over,
of a snapping turtle
I'd seen as a boy, who rose
from a muddy bog to glimpse,
I'd imagined, the sky,
the moon and stars,
before dipping its head under,
carrying the mat of algae
and moss on its battered shell,
drifting down to burrow back
into the muddy bottom,
into more algae and moss, to await
the silvery flash of frog or fish.

"THE AS USUAL DANCE TOWARDS THE OTHER FLIGHT TO WHAT IS NOT, PARTS 1 & 2": A POETICS OF AVOIDANCE

after Fred Frith

I'm trying to understand what it means
to drift oblivious through all these years. I'm trying
to see where the self-improvement goes.

I'm brushing my hand across my forehead.
I'm listening to music that aspires
to the sound of travel or pain

or the pain of travel—a repetitive guitar figure
that sounds like waiting or walking,
the *chunkachunk* clatter of something being

rolled or started or tested, the ping of someone
laying a metal hammer to something
also made of metal, the *brrrt* of voltage,

then everything falling apart at once.
I'm thinking this will be a poem if it can avoid
being an essay, a song, a long walk

through the arbor where the grapes
are achieving a deep powdered purple
and bees are loud and quick in vapor-thick air.

I should mention my wife is pulling weeds
in the hot sun but that would make this
a confessional poem and drag me

straight into the waters I am always
already standing hip deep in—the legacy
of secrecy and deceit and yes, friends,

avoidance. Notice how the diction
turns abstract here. The administration
would like to tender its sincerest

apologies to all parties that might have been,
let us say, "injured" by said administration's
impulsivity. We would like to say

that such matters will be addressed
in a closed-door session after the video,
after the guitar that sounds

like a slammed door and the other
guitar that whimpers like a monkey
and the three guitars that have given up

making any of the various rumbles
and twangs the guitar was invented to make,
have stopped. Description, too,

is a kind of avoidance.

EVENING, MILAN, FASHION WEEK

Out of nowhere they appear,
Stilting into alleys

Easing across barricades,
Arms tanned and inked, calves

Muscled and lean,
A cadre of leggings,

A clatter of heels,
Silk like a breeze caught

And spun 'round their necks.
Faces drawn; skin, pellucid.

Hair fountained
Or shocked tall. Too

Ragged to join them,
The old man peers, plain

As a pigeon, ballcap
And sweatshirt, rough beard—

A hush of denim
Amid the elegant din.

A CATECHISM

What is this silence?

The ache of the arc
of the finch's flight.

And the body?

An inexplicable yearning,
sunlight slick on birch bark.

Your darkest secret?

Dappled pony. Pied sycamore.
Stippled light under the maple.

Your greatest joy?

Harbored in the music,
she danced alone,
in the dark, by
the ladies' room door.

And greater still?

The Cooper's hawk
stirring up finches
and sparrows like a dog
let loose among chickens.

And yet you walk, slumbering,
among the things of the world.

Having seen, these eyes
can no longer see.

If you were to wake fully,
what would you witness?

Heidegger, who loved
poetry and yet ...

Could you fall in love again
with life, with living?

The mid-May tractor would be
a raucous hymn to possibility.

We all die. Why
is your death important?

Johnny darters in the drainage pond;
kingfisher in the dying elm.

What do you expect will happen after?

Hurt, it seems, lives in the flesh,
inviolate, permanent, untouchable.

And the soul?

Gravel crunch, thump
of clutch pedal,
hymn of tires on asphalt.

And god?

Lights flashing over you
where you slumber
in the back seat.

MONK'S CRUSH

All the hurts inside all the hooks

And the impossible note

Not even spinning not even the minor second

When the ringless hand flashes

From the bass line to hack the trouble

Not rage but joy an electrical surge

Saying wreck this then make it beautiful again

Tip this then set it right again

All the hooks inside all the hurts

A muttered need a quick complaint

Arpeggio of want

Suspended, augmented, unadorned

Hitch in his gait hitch in his rhythm

He must have heard it everywhere

Felt it in the hurtling the hurting world

Slip step whirl dodge and duck

Nellie dressing him and he can't stop turning

PHOTOGRAPH: PRISON CAMP, IRAQ, 2003

You can see the depths they are avoiding.
You can glimpse them when they look up,
raise their heads and for an instant recognize
their dire predicament. Then the meaninglessness
rolls in, rolls over them. "There is no order
in the world," said the old man, "save that
which death has put there." And, lacking
the prospect of death, they circle, wear paths,
become ironic in their pacing. That they are
difficult to spot is a tic. That they are
ghostly presences. That they are no longer
men. That the sign describes some other beast.
That when they howl in the dark, halftrack
and Humvee mutter back a sordid rumble.
That the night has been vacated. In the cold dawns
they wake and stretch, and memory shivers down
the length of their bodies. Memories of fear
and the hunt. Memories of steppe, jackal and rabbit,
of rush and tear—a quickness in the tamarisk.
Then a half-pleasant vagueness, shimmering at first
along the chain link, settles over everything.
The alertness gone, the tenseness gone
from muscled legs. Everything already settled—
grasses and *nakhla* stumps, sparrows
and finches perched in the chainlink, golf carts
already humming along the paved paths.
Man is the most philosophical of beasts,
and these who snarl and snap

briefly at the tossed meat are made sophists
of the panorama, existentialists of the hole,
wizened utilitarians at the cavemouth. Emblems
of the unsayable become sayable. Named *man*
and therefore wrung of mannishness. Known.
Settled. *They cannot, in their vulnerability,
be returned to the wild.* Their habit to be vigilant,
suspicious. Longing only to be roused
from their slumber, wanting the tremor
in the limbs when the condor
drops from its perch, hops once,
casts its cold glance, dips its unfeathered
head into the slick dark cave of the ribs.

CHOOSE YOUR OWN AMERICA

You can choose the forefathered one,
all beard and stovepipe, folderol
and feather, all foppish at the brothel.
Or that earlier one, all lunge and gallop,
musket and scatter, belfry and blunderbuss.
Or the gangrenous and stooped one, caterwauling
on the White House lawn. You can choose
the haunted one, nightshakes, the guilt-worn
and riddled, still moaning in the willows.
Or the exuberant one, the one that prances—
gray squirrel on an electrical wire,
all pomp and reflex, tail toss and brass.
Then there's the worried one, furtive
in the hovel, the duckers and shamblers,
scriveners of the mud's cursive. Or the America
of duplicates and editions, of ranch houses
and khakis, quick pledge and the concrete walkway.
You can choose the America of granite,
of cobblestone, of quick strike and vanish.
Or the America of *gracías* in the market,
miigwech on the subway, never mind
the sleek traders on the balcony, the champagne
they drizzle on the occupying hordes below.

DRIVING UTAH

after Richard Hugo

Only a Mormon could dream this Eden.
Thirty miles from Price, the hills
Are worn as miners' wives who toil
On stoves scraped blue from the tired chafe

Of pot and skillet. Still the flat screen
Rages. The boys have grown
Into larger boys and faster,
Whose thunder crack and clatter

Cheers the men worn smooth by labor,
Like stones the river and centuries own.
Departure is the last remaining cash crop.
The tourists drop just long enough

To know that they can't stay.
Even the river slinks eastward here,
Quarrying bones from sandstone.
When the last cottonwood collapsed,

They carved a playhouse in the hollow
And capped it with a roof.
There's laughter there—
Until the church bells clang.

Eighty years and gone, the old men say.
No outlaws in the Outlaw Tavern,

No lovers crowd the Pillow Talk Motel.
When whimsy strikes they call a meeting.

The cliffs rise steep to wall out meth,
Those wiry, pale pierced girls, a world
Of trouble, freedoms no one needs.
Black Mesa gavels home the grim.

THE GIFT

It begins back before memory, begins in stories told and heard, of gravelpit, hog farm, of hogs shifting in ramshackle enclosures, storm doors and logs and skids, scavenged and stacked and tied together to trap the hungers inside, to keep them in the slop and stagger, huffing and grunting there, those shadows patrolling the nights, great breathings chuffing inside the marrow pit.

It begins with the hogs, though he never saw the hogs, not with eyes that see and name and remember, not with eyes that knew "hog" and "slop" and "chuffing."

It begins there as it must, there where he was carved from oblivion, hollowed out and filled again in darkness and mud, in stomp and roll, in wild grunting and slaughter.

This part he was innocent of. This part was done, not chosen. This part he would suffer and slog through.

And had it been a field of lambs instead? Then lamblike he'd be leaping. But he was given muddle and plod, the blind belly-push, the wriggle and flop. Given hoglight. Bristle and grist. Bucketclang, snorting, and the plunging darkness.

LIMINAL

Caught by the wellhouse, they were.
Not *caught* exactly. Witnessed.
Encumbered thus: standing

& moaning. A combustion
among the chollas. A shiver, a tremor,
& even as it was happening

plotting to make it happen again.
Lilacs, that time of year, everywhere.
Had he known when he'd

pressed against her back
among the novels-in-translation,
he would have known where this

was going. First misery & indecision.
Then all out of proportion.
Then jonquils & mayhem.

Ristra on the kitchen door.
Blanket among the cacti.
Someone offhandedly

mentioning Dublin, the streets,
Joyce "sobbing another's name."
The books, thick & various.

One would read aloud, then the other.
Then his face between her legs.
As if sliding his tongue

along a book's crease.
Lingua. Lingual. Language.
Vulva. Labia. That lather & froth.

Mother tongue. Father tongue.
Tongue in the crease. A murmuring
that was a species of song.

A song that was a kind of joy.
A joy mixed with mud & feathers.
O hale. O hearty.

O remaindered & acclaimed.
His tongue in the crease.
The marvel of that.

Skin soft as the fragrance,
in humid heat, of lilacs.
The nighthawks, at sunset,

sculling like languid swallows
over the cattails. But how
to live under this sky, these stars.

Fragrance of lilacs & slumbering bodies.
Wake then. Taste everything.

This smooth black pebble.

That aspen branch.
While fireflies flash, liminal
in their slumber among grasses.

(A prolonged darkness.
A momentary brightness.
A combustion among the chollas.)

LINGUAL & FRAUGHT

Dawn like a starter's pistol. Goldfinches arcing through mist-scarved air, chattering on the updraft. All the rancorous and squalling days. Implacable days. Days of needs flashing into our lives. Days spent huffing under the quilts. Startled in the vestibule. Quickened by the chaise. Feted in the dark. Commended. Championed by the X-backed frogs. The little ones, no bigger than a thumbnail, leaping in the jewelweed, choiring in the elms. A glitter of moments flung against the darkness. Hours slipping past. Carp swirling in the mudhole. Your brother's face changing into a map of the moon. When the katydids come they come. When the katydids sound their cacophony, their symphony, their endless creaking in the tall grass. And the moths around the porch light, those dizzied scooters, raveled and powdered. Who knew they were a metaphor? I would like to speak earnestly on the occasion of. On the cusp of the nothing we were always destined for. What did we do with our days? Ideas following us like a cloud of gnats. Everything filed under "Wisdom, unburdened of." Words placed end-to-end and fiddled with. A puddle of bones and flesh. Can you make them stand up and walk? Can you breathe into them and make them breathe? In the dark, under the imaginary creatures we invented? We ran and laughed until we were tired. We slept and dreamed. Animals accompanied us everywhere. Snakes in the rockpile, salamanders swaggering on their tender legs, tanagers in the mottled sycamore. Orioles slipping into their silver purses. The lichened nest of a hummingbird, two eggs like pale peas. Barn owl, imperial ghost of the hayloft, haunting and haunted. The waxen impossible plumage, the swiveling head. Eyes that let nothing in.

EDITOR

This new Editor lacks the volume of previous versions. Even with the distortion at 10, the tones are dulcet. Even the obligatory howling has about it a classical quality, as though it were being produced by a water-damaged harpsichord. That none of the attachments fit properly, that the cord retracts like a cobra slipping through reeds, that its tasks are done with gusto but to little effect, that even as the tsunami curled beachward it was bent to the keyboard, weighing the merits of Old Goudy versus Palatino—all seem to us now minor defects. We regret our recent call to the 800 number, regret, too, our litany of complaints. The one about the nervous tapping on the TV tray. The one about the obstinate gaze sky-ward. The one about the furtive scumbling in the cash drawer. We now recognize the addition of the MP3 player as an unexpected bonus, not a flaw as previously reported. We see that the skyward gaze, rather than a failure of articulation, is actually a gesture of hopefulness, of piety even. That our communications seem often to dissolve into a wordless vapor is balanced by the addition of the LED that assures us our merest tremblings are being registered—at least if the VU meters can be trusted. While we are reluctant to subscribe to the periodic updating serv-ice, we have decided to keep our Editor, though we have stationed a sen-try to monitor its activities that seem at times to be reacting to something subliminal, something only the dogs are hearing, out at the edge of town, where the landfill ends and the reservoir licks its irradiated shores.

PROOF SHEET: AUTHOR'S PHOTO

1.
In this one taken in near darkness
you are trying to hide, trying to say *not me*,
trying to disappear, trying to project
the chiaroscuro of unknowability.

2.
In this one, head tilted, seeming affable,
chin tucked, seeming pert, seeming
agreeable, a chum or coffee date, an unseemly
seemliness, a delighted choir of seeming.

3.
Austere in this one. A professor of facticity.
A beholder of the bitterest, the most
ineluctable horrors: A wounded child, one arm
in shreds, wandering the smoke-blackened city.

4.
Happy for no reason in this one, shot
on the steps of the courthouse. In slightly
oppositional flannel while the suits circulate,
dragged by their unruly briefcases everywhere.

5.
Here, "striding purposefully." Instructed to.
The furrows thumbed from your brow.
In the tradition of Whitman—elegiac, robust,
lanky as your long-lined poems.

6.
Here you are leaned against an oak—
the ragged bark, a lilt of sunlight—holding
a sheaf of poems, inadequate crenellations
against the enshrined despoilers and plunderers.

7.
Now huddled with a mug in the wood-paneled bar.
Backed against the wall. We can almost feel
the poem assembling itself inside you—a list
of everything you oppose and are quietly becoming.

MONK PLAYS ELLINGTON

Calm but wrong. The cruelest the cruelest this
April this Paris. What now? Light drizzle. Pleasant stroll.
Lovely the gray sky and the lean woman who walks
ahead then behind, the long black coat she breathes
into the fur collar of. He is the bass climbing the keyboard.
She is the sway, blue note, minor second, the clash
of similars. The note inside the minor second—
if Monk could make it sound make it sound make it
resolve these separate fidelities, these privacies,
these solitudes among others, but he can't and when
he finally does begin "Solitude"—the single note runs,
the left hand reticent, more like a shadow falling
across the keyboard than an actual hand, the woman
begins to—she's warning the man to keep his distance.
His distance, we say, not hers. Then, in the film
I've imagined, she becomes the "sophisticated lady"
and the man eases alongside her. Blonde she is now
in the sunlight simmering through threadbare clouds.
They pause and lean together. Because it's the fifties,
and because she doesn't yet have a language for her needs,
she lets go of whatever slight she felt. He lights
a single cigarette they pass back and forth taking
turns smoking and talking. "Mood Indigo" now,
where each measure is a question, *splash of jasmine*
in a windowbox? assembly of tulips along a stone wall?
each measure a question, each flower a wish each
flower a wish, a wash, a window now flashing, rippling,
the promiscuous sun everywhere, everywhere at once.

BREEZE

He was the face of the patriarchy.
They were the women who multihandedly
summoned the Mississippi River
to appear in its concrete catacomb.
Who ran for 8.3 yards per carry.
Whispered that Smiths song into a room
blasted by microphoned assent and blather.
He was the face of the patriarchy.
In the beskywayed city. Amongst
the cartwheeling multitudes, the thronged
boulevards, the bagpipes and sermons,
the phenomenological poets displaying
their erudition, if you will, from the main stage.

He was the face of the patriarchy.
They were set to schmooze, set to irony,
set to launch and guzzle. Barge
and dazzle. Set to contend and side-bitch.
They turned slapdash at the crosswalk,
irreverent at the chapter meeting,
indignant when the dignified dipped
their faces to the trough. He was
the face of the patriarchy, formulating
his demands. They were night and snowfall
and a skirmish on the banco.
A sudden breeze in a room
built so no breeze might enter.

FASHION REPORT

Was it a shirt in or a shirt out age? No one knew for certain. It was clearly not a rolled pants era, though a few, in isolated moments, mistook it for one. It was not a blue eye shadow and pink lipstick era, that seemed clear. White calf-length boots? No. Arching eyebrows drawn severely on with a chunk of fire-hardened charcoal? *Nyet*. Was it a straight flat hair epoch? Or a soft fluffy curve around the edges of the face moment? Opinion on bangs or the vasty open sheen of the forehead was mixed. Even the experts seemed divided on whether it was the power stiletto or the innocent wonder of the flip-flop. Could the two exist side by side? Editorials in the major periodicals suggested this was unlikely. And the CPO, the Nehru, the various vestments of oligarchy? Consigned, it would seem, to the thrift shops, but beginning, again, a secret assault from those bunkers. Was this a sign of discomfort with the wars or an embrace of the ranks and charges therein? A secret army of ragtag missionaries from the marijuana-growing loft dwellers? Or simply a love of the smart epaulets, the slimming effect elicited by the clean lines of the militaristic? Such questions were remanded to the authorities for further study. Experts were quite sure it was not a loose open collar and thick silver chain era. Nor was it a button-down era, though some pressed for such a shift. It seemed that it was neither the wide tie and suspenders of rising markets nor a thin-tied rejection of traditional monetary policy. Glasses were incoherent, reflecting a certain befuddlement among the populace. Was it a subtly ambitious and slightly ironic wire-rimmed moment or did this age call for the thick black rims of realpolitik? The electrical taped bridge of solidarity seemed entirely absent from the optic landscape. The recent outbreak of irony among T-shirt slogans introduced uncertainty into the market forecasts. Even the hairstyles, mixed as they were from buzzcut to bouffant, proved unreliable as indicators. At parties, the frisson of off-the-grid patchouli mixed easily with upwardly-mobile Chanel, scuttling all attempts to read consumer confidence. Were we approaching an age? Was the incoherence a sign? And why now this incoherence, this unseemly recklessness among the wearers of clothing? And why these snappy chapeaus, when all the experts had predicted bare heads and baseball caps? Where were our vestments taking us? What would be the human cost?

AMORES PERROS

" . . . al borde del abismo."
–Guillermo Arriaga

The woman on the screen is screaming now bloodied
            palms slapping the window the prints
the slurred the parrot-like squawking the moans gurgling
            up from her throat, the doors locked.
Each time they crash the lives the storylines
            intersect. Who are

these people? *Only when*
            they are broken will we know. What woman what
white dog what siren flaring in and out of time? *Don't*
            forget her the soundtrack is saying the camera
pulling away like a sullen lover the woman's dog whimpering
            into the window the camera the audience gathered the
                                                darkness tensed

the seconds drifting through it—
            the waves and around them the shuffling the slender man uneasy
the woman leaned away into a fearful privacy
            unrestrained now sobbing sobbing—
And the man the white-haired the assassin El Chivo
            with his beloved strays drifts undetected. The voltage

flows through him—the plans the plot—
            like an announcement no one hears anymore a price check
a special offer
            a monotone spoken

through a torn speaker
        until it seems distant as god's voice.

I'm hearing in the undertones the warning that everything is aligning. I'm
                                                                    hearing
        in the spinning wheel on the overturned car. I'm leaning
to the screen whispering. I'm saying to the screen
        saying *don't* saying *stop*
because I don't know yet
        that what comes next is the bleak

groundwork.
        But do not El Chivo while no one is looking slip the brute dog the
                                                                    killer dog
into your cart . . .
        Consequences lurk in the shadows pool in the spilling gasoline—
while the onlookers
        (their hands flapping helplessly)

gather for the third time
        at the same crash
contributing only their gaze the weight falling equally
        on the cars the flames the woman—
until the bloody boy is spilled
        writhing on the pavement.

This man
        has a machete he says this one
an extinguisher. The white-haired
        the wild-looking the homeless El Chivo has stolen

the money the billfold he is unsealing his fate
        saving the brute the nearly dead killer dog.

Already we can feel his beloved strays
        Flor Frijol Gringuita limp and bloodied in his arms.
Because it's his story now his turn
        to make choices
and suffer. "You want
        to make God laugh tell him your plans." Susana has already said it.

Now El Chivo is making plans. In this world where every longing
        turns to greed or lust turns to blood in the alley.
He has already left his wife and daughter
        already fought in the jungles
for an unrealizable ideal already killed
        for money because it's what he knows.

And the killer dog is teaching him about death
        the consequences—the innocent strays
dead and bloodied in the abandoned warehouse.
        He will wear his cracked and taped glasses
again. He will set brother against brother
        and let them face it

their gazes falling on the pistol—
        the mystery in their hearts a darkness
howling in the gap between privacies.
        While El Chivo pastes photographs
of his own face over his daughter's
        stepfather's face.

Soon he will shave and put on the suit and tie
        break into his daughter's apartment
line her sofa with bundles of cash. He will call her
        message machine from beyond the grave
spilling his story his tears.
        Then he will wander out with his dog

named *Negro* now
            through the aisles of scavenged car parts
away from us
        then suddenly toward us—
over the oil-black and fissured
        the smoldering earth—

THE CLIFFS OF MOHER

The man in the orange jumpsuit, guided by the voice
In his ear, is rehearsing, is picking his way along
The moss slick cliff edge, which is a metaphor
For nothing, for the nothingness of death,

Or the imagination's deathlessness, the vaunted,
Mossy dream of life forever that pulls him,
That emboldens him, names all of this *rehearsal*
For an afterlife, that other vocation, that calling,

Evocative now in the fricatives of courage,
Bold dream of launch and the tumbling away
Or toward, forevering past the crags and spires,
Rooks and gulls knifing in the imagined mist

He mistakes for the humid drift of heaven's inner
Chambers as he spirals toward the rock-hard ocean,
Bright tumbler in the dawn, emptied of all
Human striving, emptied, too, of courage

And fear, the *vox humana* of wind in his ear now,
The new day dawning as he lets go of *day* and *dawn*,
The hollow chamber of *this life this flesh this leap*, the voice
In his deepest ear all he needs of heaven now and earth.

THE ISLAND

Gray and fog-draped the island
    loomed legendary in firelight
        a gathering against death and cold a village

we were forbidden to return to
    by elders who had grown ashamed
        of their old lives their dances

the language they'd spoken before
    the planet's thin garment
        of *civilization*

enticed them to stand up
    in the liminal in the dreamlight
        and build a flimsy shack

of reason a raft of the sensible
    and they stopped seeing
        cormorants skimming the waves

gaunt herons in the tideflash
    barnacled whales lunging
        gape-mouthed at herring and krill

stopped eating the foods
    they'd broken apart with their hands
        and pressed to their faces

smearing their cheeks alive
        in the grease and swale of it
                in the sky and sea of it

in the spume of things
        in the litter of shells the wrack
                and pulse of oblivion

WESTERN CIV

pre-dawn, St. Pierre des Champs

Whatever owls and storks inhabit this town are still. No nightingales warble and trill. I cross the meadow and the Orbieu River and climb toward the stone and shuttered town. My own sharp footsteps. A few thin lights. No traffic. No one but me out walking. It occurs to me that I don't know the dangers here. But they've had centuries to clear the landscape of poisons, shoot the dangerous animals and display them in the town square. And by now the race of evil men John Locke wanted to protect us from has surely been reduced to a reclusive, shamed population on an island somewhere. The night is mostly a dark vagueness. The night is mostly imagined, a thin cobblestone street curving between stone buildings. Buildings built and rebuilt and added to. The layers of history. The shop now a bed & breakfast, the pasture, a campground. Mostly, though, a settled beauty: narrow streets, houses, an occasional lit window, lace curtains, nobody awake reading Proust on the divan or slicing truffles and parmesan in the kitchen. Where the road edges the river, an engine idles, three men smoke and talk softly, in utter darkness.

NOVELIST

Affable, he is, galumphing about the ranch in galoshes, his three-legged dog leaned to the bog water, the peregrine hunched like a pigeon under a cloud of ravens. He can neither be turned on nor entirely off, such is the new circuit board. He putters, then dodders, then mucks about. Like a three-legged wolfhound, he lurches toward a horizon of letters. Or cottonwoods scratching their names in a frozen sky. The grail indecipherable, the mysteries like a mist over the morning pond. The mountain fog unravels. Sunlight startles the talus slope. Two elks gallop stride for stride through the mountain meadow. They hoist the anvil off his heart, cleat it, leave it hanging. That his writings are traced in window frost. That his reputation rests on the tracks along the creekbed. That the peregrine launching itself, inauspicious as a shuttlecock, toward the aspens seems an emblem for his later years. That the thin wire of grief, the ligature that connects the past and present, is fraying. That the moment wants to swallow him, unravel the narrative. That when he spreads his arms and breathes deeply, he feels the wordless world entire. That comfort. That threat.

THE GOLDEN WIRE

Up steps he blows chromatic now,
From *rictus* to *raucous* to *ruckus*—
The center everywhere, the tonic
Just another wheezing stop on 7th Ave.

And he changes 7th Ave—hissing buses,
The gin & tonics stirred in window seats,
The ruckus a momentary tonic
For the anomie of brick and chrome.

The anonymous drummer picks up brushes
Now. The tenor's too kind, the critics say,
For greatness. He gins up a little humor
And kids the bass man 'bout the changes—

That bus was chugging into Bed-Stuy, kid,
When you showed up in Queens.
But your kind can muddle through, he cracks.
The bass man's white face brushed now

With red, his thin white fingers walk
Back through the subtle modulation,
The tenor showing him, counting it off,
While a bus boy slinks among tables.

In the shadows, the young white women slink
Or perch, flash leg on barstools, the tenor
Of the room shifting, modulating
Until a white spot settles on the singer

Who lately slunk from shadows, settled
Like a day laborer in a rooming house
On the barstool her boyfriend carried
To the stage. The shadows the spotlight

Carves beneath her eyes stage
A small rebellion in her smile that carries
The trace of every room she's ever
Nodded off in, shadowed by the pills

And needles, her own off-key warbling
In some long-forgotten set. The room stills
When she starts quietly, quelling the rebellion
In her voice now, the one time staged there,

Time and the fame that couldn't score her
Even a decent meal. Upstart, they called her,
Who couldn't get a seat in this same room
She needles with the golden wire of her song.

WAKING FROM WAKING FROM A DREAM

I could not breathe.
No matter how deeply I inhaled—
a thin wheeze of air.
I was living in a tiny apartment,
a wooden box with a single window
that overlooked a narrow
rose-filled park
that had been a highway
before the earthquakes.
In the dream I was leaned
out the window, trying
to breathe, when I woke
from what I understood
was a dream of not
being able to breathe.
The physics of it escapes me still.
Waking from the dream
was no different than dreaming,
except I could breathe.
I clattered down the stairs,
out into the bright day.
In the park, I noticed
a woman struggling to breathe.
Her toddler daughter,
too, was wheezing.
I hurried to them.
You're asleep, I said. *Wake up,*
I said. And the mother

looked at me, uncomprehending.
Wake yourself up! I said,
almost shouting this time.
And she did, or seemed to,
and her breathing cleared.
Together, we woke
her daughter. Then
we walked through the park.
Everyone was wheezing—
the homeless man asleep
under the slide, the old woman
waiting for a bus, her purchases
gathered at her feet like children.
Wake up, we said to each of them.
And then wake up again
to the homeless man who
thought, because he'd sat up,
that he was already awake.
And we continued,
the woman and her daughter
and I, to wake people.
In the burger joint
we approached a table
of wheezing diners.
Wake up! we said.
And the man looked at us
incredulously, saying,
I'm eating a damn burger.
This is as awake as I get.
There's another level,

the woman said. *There's more.*
But the man continued
wheezing, while his wife
and child heard us and woke
and breathed easier. We began
to understand that we had not
been dying, we'd been
dreaming. It became a kind
of sermon then, with each of us
taking turns preaching it.
All we have to do
is wake up, we preached.
All we have to do is breathe.

BRIEF

Ancylostoma braziliense

You arrived eager, full of expectation,
But I was a dull host, neither ripe flesh
Nor fodder, and you drifted and probed,
Divining a vacant chemistry. Absent
Of your absinthe, I was poor meat.

What you'd wanted was something else.
What you got was too much human.
Your path, a meandering red line.
Aimless, aware your time was brief, you
Swerved in the russet of your conundrum.

Did I entice, encourage? Very well,
I enticed. You, who would have—
Had I been elsewise—set spur to flesh
And got purchase on a future. I regret
The role I played in that deception.

Like a cat, I leaned in the sunny tropics,
And you mistook me and launched
Your sally. I was wrong for you;
You, wrong for me. But there was
No escape. I stopped you then—

Your misery which seemed the brink
Of pleasure—and felt your fluttering,
Lurching trip to nowhere cease. Old

Companion, I miss you, though even now
Cannot parse symptom from disease.

MONK & TRANE

The applause starts like a hard rain from a lone cloud—
a clap, another, a small burst, then the quick deluge.
And Monk starts out like that, too—a light dance
on the keys, then a downpour. He lays out twenty
possible routes, any one of which Bud might drive
from Harlem to KC. But Monk turns away
each time because this is "Monk's Mood" and he's
decided, at first, to refuse embellishment,
refuse the expected trill, filigree, grace note. He's looking
for heft, for steadiness, an anchorage—like Nellie
who straightens his collar, points him towards the piano,
shoving him off into the night like an old rowboat
from a rickety dock. He's just gotten his cabaret card back,
having taken the rap for Bud in Harlem. And Trane
has just kicked, cold turkey, in Philly, *A Love Supreme* already
building, like a new kind of muscle, in his body. And Monk,
though he succumbs to the black-tie occasion with too many
"cocktail runs" and throws the audience a bebop bone,
remains true, mostly, to himself, to the Rocky Mount
train tracks, gospel and the blues, to the underserved intervals,
the improbable voicings, the acrobatic loops.
He could play silence better than most people could play notes,
and sometimes, even tonight, he does. It's mostly
Trane's show, though in the best moments
they hit the highway together, top down, old 66,
cruising. But there's something in the trunk,
and you can hear it banging around back there,
between the tire iron and the spare, and when they

slow it down, when they pull off the roadside
west of Memphis and get out to stretch among
the glass and chrome, the windblown wrappers,
they can hear the meadowlark's chromatic runs,
the redwing's lounge trill, the steady snare and ride of traffic,
half of it going east, half west. Sweet and lovely, isn't it,
to be sober and working. Trane bringing the sweetness,
playing the straight man. Monk free to joke and quip.
Smartly dressed, ties and jackets, shades, the two of them
leaning on each other to break into a new life,
the trooper behind them already hitting the lights.

POET 65

This new, "improved" Poet baffles us. We had hoped Poet 65 would be as compelling as Poets 1 through 64, as we have enjoyed the innovations, while also admiring the apparent continuity, a recognizable "Poetness," if you will, of each successive incarnation. Compelling, we often said, certain that the compulsions were real, though what she compelled us to do remained a mystery. But Poet 65 lacks, what? The florid, the fecund laugh still erupts unremittingly, as before, and the ability to encapsulate our faults into a pithy apothegm remains. This Poet also retains the ability to improvise a mordant encomium over drinks at the St. Francis Bar after midnight. Poet 65, like the many Poets that preceded her, will often fill a water glass with vodka and swirl it in her hand as if to mix the vodka with, apparently, more vodka. It cheers us to see this trademark gesture retained; however, we miss the hand plunged to the elbow into a bag of pork rinds that marked Poets 17 through 23 and the sudden smirk that would cross the face of Poet 46, the model that came to be known as Cynical Poet and was quickly recalled, resulting in the overly solicitous Poet 47, which, I'm sure you'll remember, was roundly rejected for reasons that should be obvious. While many of us admire the balance, the steady hand at the rudder of this dinghy you call Poet 65, we miss the foreboding cutter that would sweep through the harbor at night, its radar swinging, its machinery bleeping and blinking, its armaments poised, the commands from the bridge slicing through the fog like the post-midnight yowlings of mating cats. We have read the literature accompanying this new improved Poet, and have decided to trust your predictions about the various tightenings and loosenings we can expect, the rich sonorities and overtones that will come with age, though the incessant creaking and wheezing has become an issue for some, who miss the "sleep mode" so prominently featured in the promotional materials for Poet 64. Why was such a popular feature not retained in this new "improved" Poet? We must confess—more than once we have repackaged our Poet 65, stood her in the original shipping carton and poured buckets of Styrofoam nuggets over her, only to be drawn to something—an indefinable . . . *bereftness* we had not noticed before. Each time, we have lifted her back out of the carton and plucked the static-charged nuggets from her vestments. And so she remains, wandering the house in darkness, like a light we wish we'd turned off, a light that wakes us just enough that we remember our dreams, dreams about men lost in the jungle, the vacant foundations of houses, charred timbers and smoldering sofas, before we slide back under the slick black unrippling surface of sleep.

ON DISAPPOINTMENT

After the prizes were claimed, the medals tilted to glint
In the spotlights and flashbulbs. After the certificates
Were signed and framed, the speeches hinting
At dark political maneuverings obliterated

By the weary orchestra. After the nominees and runners-up
Were ensconced and limousined. After the last
Eligible contestant had tucked her program into her purse,
The shame of once having hoped searing her cheek—

The prideful strut, the rented dress, the shoes,
The tendered preparation for the snub. And the man gone,
So accustomed to failure that he dressed like the walls
Themselves, like the wait-staff that whisked away,

First, the punch bowl, then the squandered cake,
The plates and forks, the flutes, the towel-wrapped Prosecco
Aslant in its tepid bucket. After the winners were toasted,
Encomiumed, vaunted. After the best were declared, and the list,

No matter how many times they ran their fingers down it,
Did not include their names, how did they continue?
When the resources for continuance were denied them,
How did they continue? Oh, tenderest outsiders,

You who huddle in vestibules waiting to be recognized,
Apprised and embraced, admired, mobbed, *Lie down again*
Where all things start, in the foul rag and bone shop of the heart.
In blessed obscurity toil and render there the battered doll,

Abandoned toolshed, bandana-ed workers leaned
Against a sun-scorched van. When the low sun gilds
The wheatfield, lighting up each spike, each stem and tiller,
Medals will begin to tarnish, ribbons fray and flutter,

Until all is dulled by rain and wind, every glinting thing.

THE POET

He washed ashore one August. Two fishermen dragged his dripping body to the square. They propped him against the monument to their esteemed founder. A small crowd gathered. The town librarian put her hand under the man's chin, lifted his face. *It's him!* she said. *The poet!* The village constable slapped the poet's face. The poet moaned. He raised one hand and waved it like a drunk shooing a bothersome fly. Then his hand fell and his head tilted. *He's dreaming,* someone said. *Of lost love,* someone added. *Wake him up!* the constable shouted, *before he commits a poem!* The cook from the village's only restaurant came out of the kitchen, wiping his hands clean on his apron. The cook summoned his dishwasher, who lugged a pot of cold water into the square, tossed it on the poet. The poet did not respond. Therefore, did the mayor declare him *Poet Laureate of the Village.* Two stonemasons stopped working and held the poet up while the mayor read the proclamation. When they set him back down, a family of tourists gathered around him. The father put his arm over the poet's shoulder. The mother took a photograph. The four-year-old girl with oceanic blue eyes sat beside him, looking up as if she were hearing a magical story of high seas and voyages and improbable creatures with flippers and tusks. Her mother took a photograph. The photograph was published in the village newspaper. Soon, everyone was traveling to the village, posing for photographs with the poet. A woman cuddled with him, pretending they were lovers spending a romantic weekend at the shore. She sent the snapshot to her ex-boyfriend. A man pulled a Packers T-shirt over the poet's head, placed a backwards baseball cap on him, put a beer in his hand. A fisherman's widow gathered her four children and sat for a family portrait, poet as father. The Chamber of Commerce had a moustache painted on his face, a beret tilted jauntily on his head. An amorous woman pulled her shirt up and pulled his face to her breasts.

Her girlfriend pulled his face near her crotch, smiling provocatively into the camera. In this way, the poet continued living. But part of him was still stroking through a storm-tossed sea, waves rising mountainous around him, a poem churning in his chest like the light from an unreachable lighthouse.

GRAIL

This freedom is not academic. It thrusts long
In the ephemeral darkness and tumbles
To the slaughterhouse floor. Then emptiness
Opens its arms once again. Though you wanted

Perhaps a scuttle of words about night and time
Or the nightmare in which you're exposed
As the flawed and flayed creatures you are,
Ridiculed by the gowned and suited grownups,

Those gloved hands applauding lightly
The sudden launch at tenderness as if
This groping darkness, the candle guttering
Finally out, this freedom you sought

And were granted by dusk and that was
By dawnlight snuffed, could, among the ten
Thousand things, the griefs and betrayals,
The gossip and grave diagnoses, bring

A cup of comfort to your cold lips. They know
They know, those dank observers
Who loosen their ties and softly cough
Into their sleeves. Caretakers of caution,

They'll retire to chenille and thread counts,
Lie smug in their laundered thoughts. Though
You wanted perhaps comfort, you got instead
This retrenchment of hope squandered

At the altar of desire, the quarrel between light
And curtain settled by one sweep of the arm.
This freedom is not academic.
It is required as night is required, seasonal

And measured. And seasoned thus, you live awhile
And die, riven evenly by loss and hope
And this thin stream of light settling now
Wholly in the grail of your own cupped hands.

MANATEES

Manatees lounging in their underwater parlors,
drifting through the long afternoons, like women
in an impressionist painting—given a Sunday, given
flowers and a rowboat, tea and lace. Manatees
in their rough hides, floating slowly over the weedbeds—
like women in the park. Or like dirigibles
in photographs, drifting through a black and white sky,
drifting toward the inevitable lashing and tethering,
one century giving way to the next, drifting
made obsolete by the churning engines, the props
turning to turbines, the quickening also in the pulse,
in the body's core, in the implicate order,
the human minds ticking in the shadows,
calculating, monitoring, the calculus of ardor
and need unscrolling into a world torqued by greed,
by cigarette boats cutting furrows in the shallows,
churning back to port, strafing the dreamy manatees,
the driver shaking his glass to cool the scotch,
the bikinied women, lovely now, lying on the deck,
lounging, turning brown and browner in the pitiless sun.

SOLSTICE

I would like to say this
night is annunciation,
that the waning moon floats
the winter sky, a wafer of light
on a tongue of darkness,
or tell you how my father
once, legend has it, pissed
in the gas tank of a '39 Ford
and rattled the last miles home,
but who knows where this
particular darkness will take us,
smuggling us in a willow basket
across the snowy fields
while Orion grabs, with one
strong arm, three rabbits by the ears,
with the other hoists
an armful of kindling, and plods
steadily across the sky. I meant
to tell you to breathe deeply,
meant to say I'll be back,
in darkness or light, meant
to say we'll lay a fire, roast
these mealy rabbits and sing
at the end of this short day a song
about light, how it comes again,
untended, regardless, hands out
in supplication, asking
forgiveness for being itself,

for being a disturbance of air
between the wings of night,
for promising us so much
that darkness finally delivers.

STATE OF THE UNION

Meanwhile, the endless marketing of insinuations:
The headphoned man, the Fox News crawl,
the economy in its blue suit, each slaughter
a selling point, each tongue slip unleashing
a delirium of pundits, a gloating, a tweetstorm,
a chance to vanquish.
                              The choices were cabernet
or chardonnay. The charcuterie was shuttered.
The engine sounded most confident—full-throated
and steady—to the passengers over the wing.
Elsewhere, a thin humming, a mosquito
in a sleeper's ear. Elsewhere, the undisciplined roar.
Elsewhere, the shifts and vicissitudes.
                              The man
and woman on the tiny screen, rebuilt
in their own image, would live forever now,
limned and animated, death bringers
in the uncanny valley. We slid over the land
as if on a thin layer of grief. The celebration
was nested inside the fatalities, the cordoned
holocaust.
                    This was the American Way,
the music seeping into the lobby like radiation.
One word for it might be *obsequious*. Another,
vainglorious. As in that caravanned orchestra
mounted on white horses that serenaded
Custer's 25th Cavalry, until arduousness
trumped ardor and they turned back.

                                                    In the soundtrack
of our days, history manifests
as fatuous strings, the fortissimo of empire
swelling, filling the silence until even the victims
are humming along. Until one black man kneels,
another begins clapping. Until a single black woman
leans back, her eyes squeezed shut
against the moment's misery, and lets loose
something between sob and howl.
                                        We live
now in that arc between signal and noise,
that sparkleap, that wail beseeching justice,
that craw-engendered cry shaped by lungs and tongue,
lips and teeth, such keening set loose in the murderous world.

ENDING ON A DRAWING BY RICHARD TUTTLE

"Nearness preserves farness."
–Martin Heidegger

Window-glance of lilacs on adobe, a light breeze and sunlight
shivering thin shadows on the wall, tulips blading up
through loam and leaf-rot. From brush-stroke and trowel-slip,

from windrow poplars leafing-out to wind-dwarfed oak,
a shadowy yet lucid history—water rushing the ditch-mouth,
rose and lilac rifted alike with mountain light and thunderhead,

with elk-bugle, bear-chuff, bolete and chanterelle, the silent rift
between first sight and pounce, the lion shadowing the straggling lamb—
like a painting that carries the heft of gold-leaf, of clay and wool,

the arched stroke of horses, golden in the mist-shrouded meadow.
We are like that newly-sighted woman oppressed by the vituperations
Of shadow, of color—the bugled blues and honking reds pressed hard

against her eyes, her ears, purpling everything—a blastula of color,
a fistula, a fist that whelms and overwhelms with newness
until the barest stroke of graphite—part line, part silence—tacks

across a flat pond of lined paper, a light hand on the tiller, buffeted
by chance, by the weight of sunlight on penstemon—a breath so
gentle now across the earlobe carrying just your whispered name.

GRATITUDE

Forget each slight, each head that turned
Toward something more intriguing—
Red flash of wing beyond the window,

The woman brightly chiming
About the suffering of the world. Forget
The way your best friend told the story

Of that heroic road trip, forgetting that you drove
From Tulsa to Poughkeepsie while he
Slumped dozing under headphones. Forget

The honors handed out, the lists of winners.
Forget the certificates, bright trophies you
Could have, should have, maybe won.

Remind yourself you never wanted them.
When the spotlight briefly shone on you,
You stepped back into darkness,

Let the empty stage receive the light,
The black floor suddenly less black—
Scuff-marks, dust, blue tape—the cone

Of light so perfect, slicing silently that perfect
Silent darkness, and you, hidden in that wider dark,
Your refusal a kind of gratitude at last.

AFTER THREE NIGHTS SLEEPING
IN THE HOSPITAL PARKING LOT

*"It is only as long as a distinction is made between real and
imaginary murders that real murders are worth committing."*
–Norman O. Brown, *Love's Body*

Here in the unprincipled heat of human devotion—
on the hospital sidewalk, a ragged man

in a Raiders cap roped to a pit bull; the homeless
woman chainsmoking and shouting at drivers;

the young woman, thin and tanned, whose future,
when it arrived, stunned her with its rapaciousness.

The security guard cruises the periphery,
though the dangers are everywhere.

All the prepositions of location all the markers—
tree frogs at daycare, neighbor's cat squalling on the fence line—

these radiate out until the news comes back
rifted with pain, the immigrant mother cuffed

in her grief, the child dragged roughly away.
When the laws are not rigid enough, we make more laws.

When the weapons are not thorough enough,
we make them more lethal. All damage

is collateral damage, intention the cruelest excuse.
The man who says I wanted to be a priest

but ended up a shooter; the woman who says
I became that violence and longed to replicate it.

The child letting the animals speak to each other
on the sunlit playground entering a terrorist's dream.

The prisoners ambling in their orange jumpsuits.
For each one, an entourage to joke with them

about boyfriends and drugs, to wrestle them
to the drear floor, while these others, spawned

of smiling parents and the privacy hedge, approach
the coffee shop's ledger of choices, credit cards

in manicured hands. On what moment does a life turn?
How does one begin again in the grasp of,

on the cusp of, in the crucible of?
What tools? What stray munitions?

If this were a deposition, a disquisition, an essay—
but wisdom is fragmented, causality

a fabric stained by chance, by the profligate moment, toads
in the barberries, a staunch accordion-music drifting,

turning the neighborhood into a kind of festival,
a May dance, a blossoming. Music can save us

until it doesn't. Art can save us until it doesn't.
Justice is a pale frog nosing through duckweed.

There's a metaphor here but you will be hard pressed to find it.
And still we turn we turn in the splendor and grace.

The stars over the parking lot, though muted by grief
and halide lights, are the same stars.

For *we* are the rough beast the desert the lake
assault rifle bullets the pierced and torn flesh

hand over mouth hard-pressed knee.
We are the muffled screams and the night,

river thick with silt and shallow bay,
black mud predator and prey, the ocean beyond—

THE EROS THAT CAMPS ON THE EDGE OF THE VALLEY OF DEATH IS THE ONLY EROS

Eros of wars and gods and the hardscrabble millions. Of pustules pox and the fire-blind saints. Of stalkers clandestine and their backlit prey. Of monuments of wet falling snow. Of car crash tire spin the calligraphy of blood.

Of darkness of the shadows inside darkness. Of napes and ears of tongues and lips. Of hair brushing warm across the back of a hand. Of teeth and nails and the hard grip. Of wrist-back knee-back depths of the eyes.

Of leaf-tremble elk-bugle the bittern's deep bellows. Of floodwaters plane crash high mountain stream. Of whiteout blizzard of snowblind and lost. Of firelight smoke-spire eyes deep in shadow. Of now now now. Of always. Of never. Of long darkness and the one bright flash.

IN THE TUMULTUOUS DAWN

In the tumultuous dawn—
    Turk's cap lilies,
        chatter of finches,
            sun-glint off the silver roof.

Unhomed by theory,
    alienated from this plenty,
        you prop the wooden palette
            against the cardboard

that holds the tarp
    to let accumulated rain
        pour off the downslope side.

Somebody's cheap boombox
    squeals and rumbles "in
        the government yard
            in Frenchtown"
                then fades.

Soon, you will storm the palace.
    Soon the tear gas.
        The LRAD.
            The water cannons.

Even this is industry.
    Even this feeds capital.
        Even your resistance is monetized.

Only the warbler flickering
in the greenery is of no consequence—
feathery nihilist in the nada
of palmetto and plume.

THE BODY IS THE SITE OF DISCIPLINE

"No moment is innocent."
—Carolyn Huber

We are formed by trauma and torment,
        a system of punishments and rewards
                (which are also punishments).

Pleasure is a kind of discipline.

Absent discipline, we languish in freedom.

Freedom is the longed-for punishment.

Nothing, the song says,
        left to lose.

Ardent among box elders.
           Squeamish in the barrow-pit.
                Sodden among sods.

We are hogs snorting through leaf-mold,
        sniffing out pleasure then
                justice then pleasure again.

When we are giving pleasure,
                        we are half dervish, half devil.

To give pleasure is to tame,
                    to make oneself indispensable.

The gaze is everywhere.

In the sun room alone, among the houseplants:
        the sun's gaze, the begonia's gaze,
                the ticking of a clock.

Everything conspires.

SOUNDINGS

In the instructions, we are warned to decide how energetic we want
our chorus to be—

Happening is not what we thought it was: *occurrence* vets even the
ridgetop plume—

Empaneled now, we can see the threat clearly—

Frogs lounging, floating, stretched just under the water's surface,
sunlight orbing the eyes, turning yellow-green all the edges
of evolution's endangered child—

The nerves carouse even in sleep, even in the stillness before dawn—

Randomness is purposeful—

He wakes in pain, his neck barely able to hold up his beleaguered
head—

Best to avoid the tonic entirely in the verse and let the tension build—

The dream arose in response to the day's events, but the talking deer
in his open palm was unexpected—

The whimsical arrives as an apparent counter to death, but death is
in everything like a secret ingredient—

Seen dispassionately, the centipede was briefly beautiful: tawny,
mechanical, precise—

A poem's articulations, its ligatures: evolved form and stentorian
        depths—

The engine of activism is often the overbearing father, the bed pitched
        and slung, the breathing—

The three-legged tomcat returned from a night hunt to lay a three-
        legged weasel on the back step—

We attempt to distinguish between the miraculous and the coincidental,
        not realizing that the miraculous and the coincidental are in-
        distinguishable—

They mined everything for meaning, as if meaning were a nutrient—

If all the memories return, she said, will I be the person I was before
        the accident and how will I know—

The star-nosed mole, fur slick and sheened, popped out of the leaf-pile
        and was briefly gunmetal-gray and beautiful and ill-made for
        travel over grass—

Your lyrics in the bridge should resolve whatever issues the verse and
        chorus raised—

About is always an illusion, a mask: so much energy given over, given
        up, given, as in this gift of quiet: the wren pausing, tilting its
        head, the cat a mirrored silence in the bunchgrass—

ODE TO THE CORONAVIRUS

Teach me how to love the cough, the test,
the social distance, canceled prom, empty gym,

the steady slide into impoverishment.
My ears, at this late age, make of silence

a steady hiss, so I'm never alone, except
with my failures. Failure to forget myself

completely for just a moment. Even as
my granddaughter swings her tiny foot—*golpe,*

golpe, golpe—I'm thinking *my* granddaughter, as if
the reckless joy she brings to the dance

is part mine. But nothing is mine. And that's
the lesson you came to teach. Everything

crumbling. Everything suspended a moment
like pollen on the water at the top of a waterfall.

Or like a stray dog in traffic, lunging & turning.
Or a bat in the bedroom flapping raggedly

toward one wall & the next. If just for one
moment I could still the hiss in my ears,

the shuddering in my chest, or call it
something else—a *shimmering*—then would I be

like the humming stones at the waterfall's foot
that welcome the weight of water & pollen:

golpe fuerte, golpe de suerte, golpe mortal.

VINTAGE

for Maxine

The singer sang a cappella for thirty seconds, then the beat dropped.
Now where were we? We kept talking about that cute thing
our granddaughter did. The kids wanted to talk about the failure
of cryptocurrency to capture the public's imagination.
Then we remembered the "kids" were thirty-something. The actual
kids were speaking a language we didn't recognize at all. We were
binge-watching our days and they were terrifying—pandemics,
deaths by cancer, inexplicable deaths, deaths of birds trembling
beside the plate glass. We kept voting for the least-offensive politician.
But we were governed by a shrill posse from up near the tree-line.
It was spring, and the finches were copulating in the peach tree
but it didn't cheer us. The skunks ambled through the arugula
like mental patients. We couldn't remember the name
of that disease that kept you from remembering. We couldn't
remember the name of the person we could call who would know.
We were googling it, typing into our phones with a single
shaking finger. Looking over then through our glasses.
All the knowledge we had acquired no longer applied—
the past tense of *lie*, where the semi-colon went, the past tense
of *lead*, how to calculate fractions, the capital of Idaho.
How had we been so wrong about the future? No jet packs
but all these algorithms. Everything extruded. Everything we loved
now *vintage*. Yet still, in isolated pockets, people were making music
on actual instruments. Still, in isolated pockets, actual food from gardens.
In the swamps, actual frogs, harrumphing in the cattails,
redwings trilling and spreading their wings, a lone heron
drifting ghostly above its ghostlier reflection, and somebody's

granddaughter hunkered in the mud, saying "wait," saying "frogs,"
just crouched and still, just listening to our vintage world.

THE BLOSSOMING DARK

1.

The glance was everywhere, humming among the projected desires—
    houses bulging with goods, Russian sage showering the
    afternoon with lavender blossoms, moon turning full and
    beautiful in our desperation.

This idea that the world was birthed from our needs. The IEDs and
    iPods. The grommets and silks. *The Great Philosophers of the*
    Twentieth Century. Potted meat. Post Office. The reconstructed
    woman sliding upside down, red heels wrapped around a silver
    pole.

The glance tangled in the trumpet vine. The vine itself. The music it
    wanted to make. An orange music. Thin as a wire. Where were
    they taking us? What bother laced our foreheads? What dialect
    of money would they speak there?

2.

In Hanoi, thousands of wires spanned the *emptiness*, the *panoply*, the
    indeterminate universe, the *wicked excess*, the *unaccountable*
    plenty, as when we traveled from floor to floor gathering
    crustaceans, noodles, ribs, chicken wings, *pho*, eel.

As when we flipped through propaganda posters from *The American*
    War. As when the rain fell, relentlessly, on the Temple of
    Literature.

3.

When the man and his three-year-old daughter sat in meditation in
       Wat Phnom, the daughter tilted her head back and rolled her
       eyes to see me and smile.

When the fire swept through the room. When the angers were
       extruded, the signals disrupted—alternately *here is the latest
       from* and *cold front* and *pit bull impounded.*

When the lights began going out in the valley, a wave of darkness
       rolled toward us.

When the computer screen in the empty room flared and dimmed,
       flared and dimmed.

When the gong.

When the colonial hotel. Vase. Single yellow flower. Mahogany
       paneling. A water glass, sweating. White petals floating in it.

4.

In Cambodia, all the poets were princes, composing new lyrics to the
       old songs, all the elections rigged.

The monetary policy presided over the charred bones of the poor.
       Lined the coffins of the wealthy.

A new word to avoid the inconvenience. A new crawl of language. An
       angle from which to see into the incontrovertible. A scope. A
       bead. A glance. A certain inevitability in the book depository.

Nobody ever said what they *did* up there. *Book depository. Grassy knoll.*
A thousand wires. How could anyone know where the error
was, especially now that the fines had exceeded the value of the
items themselves.

It's time, the man said, *to just get some weapons and take some shit.*

5.
At Angkor Wat you could trace the history from ornate Hinduism
to austere Buddhism and back. Back and forth they went.
Answering not to truth but to power.

At dusk, we scrabbled among the rubble, the huge stone Buddhas,
smiling then glowering then perfectly impassive in the
blossoming dark.

THE GHOST OF DENIS JOHNSON

Now that I'm *a shadow of my former self*,
a shade, a wanderer on this senseless
planet of regret, I've been assigned
the task of repeating myself to the strays
and outcasts, this teenaged girl,
for example, huddled on the plaza,
wrapped in the blanket some *kind stranger*
tossed her to warm his own befuddled heart.
Befuddled is not a word I used
when my feet touched the ground,
when I could lean over a hand of cards
like I'd never seen those aces, that
one-eyed jack before, and up the ante
just by appearing bewildered. But listen,
friends, I *was* bewildered, not by the cards,
or the various approximations of my fate
that I entertained while the others
shook their glasses and let the ice
fall against their teeth, but by the blur
of faces, the small miracles of companionship
I felt when the dealer slid two cards my way
and I turned up the edges, as if just peeking
would grant them the opportunity
to transform themselves into aces.
The girl on the plaza never asked
for the twenty I handed her and took it
without a smile or a word and I recognized
her then, another traveler among

the exhausted lights turned low
and the bells from the cathedral, more
gong than ring, sending their secret message
to the tourists trudging through new snow—
something about an eternal life
that girl and I were immune to, since we
were already dead and also undead,
and knew it was all the same here
where the new snow is untouched
by our passing and the parade of souls
is the same parade, the same souls
consigned to circle this plaza forever.

ABOVE THE BEJEWELED CITY

I was a guest in their house. A house
set at the lit edge of a great city. Below us
a virus was floating like dust motes
through the streets. Their daughter
had raised a jarful of butterflies—
not a jar exactly, more like a vase.
I was having drinks with them in violation
of the latest edicts from the premier.
When they weren't speaking to me
they spoke a bright guttural language
like the one you might imagine
river rocks would speak
at the bottom of a mountain stream.
At one point in the evening,
the daughter rose politely from her chair
and performed a kind of flamenco,
snaking her hands into the air as if
pulling herself through dense undergrowth.
How can I explain? The world was ending.
In the city below people were collapsing,
struggling to breathe. I didn't know why
there were fires or why smoke
marbled the sky above the buildings.
I tried to imagine individual deaths,
eyes looking out from behind glass visors,
hands reaching up to be held.
It seemed the least I could do.
We moved onto the balcony

that overlooked the city.
We brought the vase of butterflies.
Flashing red lights jeweled the streets below us.
Sirens flared and stopped and flared again.
We stood quietly in the darkness.
As I understood it, my host was
a professor of some rarely spoken language.
His wife sang cabaret songs in a local bistro.
We removed the cover of the vase
and released the butterflies.
Would you believe me if I told you
that they sprang from the jar as though
forced upward by a burst of air, and
that they did not flutter away into the night
but one by one landed on that girl
until she was covered with wings,
all gently pulsing? Oh, readers,
it was lovely there on that balcony
above the dying world. And for a moment,
I thought she might step away
and leave the butterflies hanging there
in the shape of a girl.
After a while she pointed to herself.
What's happening? she whispered.
Her parents said something
in their underwater language
that caused her to begin slowly turning,
and the butterflies began to loosen their grip
and flutter into the night,
catching the light a moment

before they were lost in the general darkness.
That is how it has always been done
in our country, my host told me.
With one such as her.
And I believed them, dear reader.
Wouldn't you have? On such a night,
in such a world—

Jon Davis has received a Lannan Literary Award, the Lavan Prize from the Academy of American Poets, a General Electric Younger Writers Award, the Off the Grid Poetry Prize, two National Endowment for the Arts Fellowships, a Lannan Residency, and fellowships to The Fine Arts Work Center in Provincetown and Cill Rialaig Artists' Retreat in Ireland. He taught for twenty-three years at the Institute of American Indian Arts before founding, in 2013, the IAIA low residency MFA in Creative Writing, which he directed until his retirement in 2018. From 2012 to 2014, he served as the City of Santa Fe's fourth Poet Laureate.

ACKNOWLEDGMENTS

I thank the editors of the following journals for publishing these poems:

"*Amores Perros,*" *Projector*

"The As Usual Flight Towards the Other Flight to What is Not, Parts I & 2": A Poetics of Avoidance," *Mississippi Review*

"Bio Note," *Guesthouse*

"The Blossoming Dark," *Waxwing*

"The Body is the Site of Discipline," *Bennington Review*

"Choose Your Own America," *The Philadelphia Review of Books*

"Driving Utah," *Thin Air*

"Editor," *Black Warrior Review* and *Verse Daily*

"Ending on a Drawing by Richard Tuttle," *El Palacio*

"Fashion Report," *The Laurel Review*

"The Gift," *Guesthouse*

"Gratitude," *Poem-a-Day*

"The Island," *Poetry at Sangam* (India)

"Lingual & Fraught," *Diagram*

"Manatees," *Poetry at Sangam* (India)

"Novelist," *Black Warrior Review*

"Ode to the Coronavirus," *terrain.org*

"Orality," *Poetry*

"Photograph: Prison Camp, Iraq, 2003," *Mississippi Review*

"The Poet," *Mississippi Review*

"Poet 65," *Black Warrior Review*

"Proof Sheet: Author's Photo," *Thin Air*

"Solstice," *Taos Journal of Poetry & Art*

"Vintage," *Bennington Review*

"Western Civ," *Poetry at Sangam* (India)

"Monk Plays Ellington," 2013 Poetry Calendar, Bertem, Belgium: Alhambra Press, 2012.

"On Disappointment" was runner-up in the 2017 W. B. Yeats Poetry Contest.

"Grail," appeared in *A Greater Sublime,* Santa Fe, NM: The Press at The Palace of the Governors, 2018.

"Monk's Crush," "Monk & Trane," and "Monk Plays Ellington" appeared in *Thelonious Sphere*, Q Ave. Press/ Iron Horse, Texas Tech University, Lubbock, TX, 2011.

"Ode to the Coronavirus," "Choose Your Own America," "State of the Union," "Brief,"
"Western Civ," "The Eros that Camps on the Edge of the Valley of Death is the
Only Eros," "In the Tumultuous Dawn," "The Body is the Site of Discipline,"
"Soundings," "Vintage," and "Above the Bejeweled City" appeared in *Four
Quartets: Poetry in the Pandemic* (Tupelo Press, 2020).

With thanks to the Lannan Foundation and the Artists' Retreat at Cill Rialaig, County
Kerry, Ireland, for the gift of time and solitude. Thanks to my teachers, Richard Geller,
Dick Allen, Richard Hugo, Patricia Goedicke, William Pitt Root, Joy Harjo, and Bill
Kittredge. Thanks to Norman Dubie and the other hundreds of poets who did not know
they were my teachers. Thanks to Sherwin Bitsui, Santee Frazier, Ken White, Joan Naviyuk
Kane, Chee Brossy, Larry Siems, Dana Levin, Arthur Sze, and, especially, Greg Glazner—
the farflung community of poets whose presence inspires and motivates me. Thanks to the
alumni, faculty, and staff at the Institute of American Indian Arts, who were at the center
of my writing and intellectual life for 28 years. Thanks to Elizabeth Murphy, Ian Hatton,
Rob Arnold, Dan Carey, Michael Alpert, and everyone associated with Grid Books. Thanks
to my partner, Teresa White, and to Grayce, Mike, Gregory, Briana, Evan, Matt, and An-
drew. And, finally, to my granddaughter, Maxine Rael Zayas, who helped carry me through
the pandemic with her love of life and animals and dance.